S0-AWO-925

Centennial Edition

A BARANGAY ACTIVITY BOOK

Pilipinas A to Z

ALL YOU NEED TO KNOW AND DO
TO BEGIN UNDERSTANDING PILIPINAS

by
Melchizedek Maraon Solis

SRMNK Publishers

Salinas, California, U.S.A.

INTRODUCTION TO THE
"Pilipinas A to Z"
CENTENNIAL EDITION

In 1898, the nation Pilipinas came into being when workers, farmers, fisherfolks and other Pilipinos, supported by their wives and even by priests, organized the Katipunan and fought against the Spaniards who had colonized the people for more than three hundred years. On September 29, 1899, sensing victory, they wrote the Constitution for a government they called *Republika ng Pilipinas*, whereby they declared to the world their will to become a free nation and people.

At that time a century ago, Pilipinos waged war against the United States just because Americans decided to take over the colonization of Pilipinas. Unlike the invading Americans who were set for war, Pilipinos were easily defeated and, as a result, Pilipinos have been struggling to shape their nation with America as a major factor of contention. That endeavor bred a bevy of heroes and is another good cause for a centennial celebration.

Pilipinos, whereever they are in the world, will profit from being reminded of those moments of valor by individuals and organizations fighting to keep what they believed had been endowed upon them by God Almighty. Strength and fresh vision are gained from rehashing ways by which people of courage responded to events so that better communities could be built. To be sure, there were deceptions, errors and failures. Horrible were the executions and massacres; ironically, those tragedies are also cradles of noble heroes.

Remembering them is a fine form of celebration because it is a proven way of providing ourselves with inspiring role models.

Looking back in order to learn and understand this national heritage is the spirit behind this revised and updated big little book. Own it, read it and share it. That's a small but celebrative, positive step to take as Pilipinas begins its journey into the next one hundred years.

Melchizedek Maraon Solis
Salinas, California
January 1999

Pilipinas A to Z

ALL YOU NEED TO KNOW AND DO
TO BEGIN UNDERSTANDING PILIPINAS

This big little book on Pilipino culture and history is a substantial appetizer. Alongside the basic information on each topic, there is a short discussion of relevant issues.

Besides leading you to the festive main course of serious study, this Barangay Activity Book provides something for you and your family, your barangay. Whenever you do the suggested barangay activities together, everyone will develop insights and communication skills that are important to the family. In a way this book believes in the saying "The family that reads together stays together."

In each essay there are sources that treat the topic in full; the reader will profit much by turning to these excellent materials for more in-depth treatment. For additional Pilipino flavor there are *salawikain* or sayings at the top of each page. At the end of the book is a Learner's Guide with an outline of the forces that are propelling Pilipinas to nationhood --- in itself, another helpful tool for studying and teaching Pilipino history and culture.

We know that after reading this book you will want to feast on more facts and fuller information about Pilipinas.

Throughout this book we use **Pilipinas**, the name Pilipinos chose as the name for their native land.

Mabuhay!

Acknowledgment

To all those involved in the conception, production and distribution of this Centennial Edition of **"Pilipinas A to Z: A Barangay Activity Book"** I express my most heartfelt gratitude, especially to the following:

The *kapatiran* in the Caballeros de Dimasalang for providing me while in the United States the most profound sense of Pilipinism with the insistent sense of responsibility for the creation of a vehicle on which elements of Pilipino heritage could be communicated to succeeding generations---for foundational inspiration, I am most grateful;

Colleagues in the Educators of Monterey County (EofMC²) and the Filipino American Educators Association of California (FAEAC) for giving me the conviction that there is a group of qualified and dedicated persons who inspire and support anyone undertaking even just a part of such an enormous task as educating the youth for the appreciation of a national heritage;

Dr. Elmira Layague Johnson and Dr. Consuelo T. Gomez, particularly, deserve highest praise for suggesting excellent changes and additions;

Friends and co-adventurers in the Filipino American National Historical Society who realize that the burden of defining and sharing the Pilipino experience is big but, by *bayanihan*, bearable;

Freshest of our inspiration---the vibrant youth from Project UGAT (United for Governance, Articulation and Travel), Central Coast California budding writers and artists with vision and power seeking their roots in history;

My *akbayanihans* in the National Filipino American Council, Monterey County Chapter (NFAC MCC)), who continue to courageously search for the means to share the riches of the Pilipino heritage, I thank you and salute you;

Leo Partible for the engaging illustrations;

And to all in my beloved *barangay* in America, notably graphic artist Melanie Solis McKnight, printing manager Ron McKnight, master prepressman Lawrence Lopez Solis and photographer Reev Lopez Solis --- for their actual, unique, personal touches in the production of this book---and most especially Mutya;

Maraming Salamat. Mabuhay!

M. M. Solis

January 1999

Table of Contents

Foreword   3
Acknowledgement   5

Archipelago   9
Barangay   11
Bisayas   13
Corregidor   15
Darangen   17
España   19
Flores de Mayo   21
GomBurZa   23
Gabriela   25
Humabon   27
Intramuros   29
Jeepney   31
Katipunan   33
Luzon   35
MetroManila   37
Mindanao   39
Narra   41
Olongapo   43
Pinoy   45
Quezon   47
Republic   49
Sabong   51
Taglish   53
Ulog   55
Vinta   57
Watawat   59
Ximenez   61
Yamashita   63
Zapote   65

Forces Propelling Pilipinas to Nationhood   66
Learner's Guide   68

8

A is for *Archipelago*

The **archipelago** known as *Pilipinas* (Americanized into *Philippines*, from Hispanic original *Filipinas*) is comprised of more than 7,000 habitable islands with an area of 300,440 square kilometers.

Archeological diggings at Tabon caves in Palawan indicate traces of human habitation and culture as far back as 22,000 years.

In 1521 Spanish explorers led by Ferdinand Magellan, after sailing for more than one year, accidentally landed on one of the islands. The archipelago was colonized and named *Las Islas Filipinas*, shortened to *Filipinas*, in honor of their king Felipe II. Based on their language, Pilipinos officially named their nation *Republika ng Pilipinas*.

The Pilipinas archipelago is at the western rim of the Pacific Ocean between Japan and Indonesia. It takes eleven hours by commercial plane from the west coast of the United States to get to Pilipinas.

Pilipinas has 22,540 kilometers of coastline, longer than that of the United States. The sea is everywhere, many Pilipinos are fisherfolks. Seafood, like fish, shrimp, squid and seaweed, is abundant. Sea products for international export is a growing industry.

Being close to the sea, Pilipinos make efficient seamen who are on demand globally as crew members for ships. During the Spanish period, Pilipinos made and fitted galleons; they were the natural and effective crew of the globe-circling vessels.

Mostly, Pilipinos farm the land for a living. When families overgrow the land, members leave home and usually go to the cities to find work. That's what happened in the 1900s when young Pilipino farm lads migrated to Hawaii and California to become farmworkers in America.

After a century of nationhood, the population of Pilipinas exceeds seventy million. With a 2.5% annual growth rate, the population, if uncontrolled, doubles every twenty years. Pilipinos are 83% Roman Catholics, 10% Evangelicals or Protestant, 4% Muslim; 3% Buddhist and other religions.

Literacy is 94%.

Islands isolate people and explain in part why, in the face of varying languages and cultures, Pilipinos have yet to achieve a more functional national unity.

Bountiful resources that come with being a sea culture need to be seen by Pilipinos as wealth for future sustainable development, not to be wasted today by exploitative and get-rich-quick schemes.

With the sea as humankind's intriguing frontier, Pilipinos half-consciously wallow in an ocean of economic opportunity.

BARANGAY ACTIVITY

Look at a map of Pilipinas and locate the hometowns of people you know. Figure distances from Manila to the U.S. and other parts of the world. Compare the size of Pilipinas archipelago to that of the State of California.

SOURCES:
   William Henry Scott,1984, Prehispanic Source Materials. Manila: New Day Publishers.
   The Philippine Islands 1493-1898, Emma Helen Blair & James Alexander Robertson, Ed., 1973. Mandaluyong: Cacho Hermanos.

Boats called *barangay* were mobile homes for Southeast Asian families as they crossed seas. Upon reaching land, they were beached to become permanent population clusters, eventually growing into self-governing political groups known, even today, as barangay.

B is for *Barangay*

Barangay is the basic unit of government of Pilipinas. Among Bisayans, the name for family is *balangay* or *banay*; the family is elemental in Pilipino life.

People lived in settlements called *barangay* when the Spaniards arrived at the archipelago in 1521. Originally, *barangay* was the name of a type of boat used by ancient Malays for crossing the seas, so that when migrating seafarers settled on land, each boatful of people was the *barangay* or the family. The typical extended Pilipino family or clan is the basic functional community.

The Spaniards found out that Pilipinos had independent barangays that oftentimes warred against each other. Magellan, in fact, was killed by Lapulapu, the chieftain of the barangay in Mactan at odds with Humabon chief of the barangay of Cebu. Despite support from the warriors of Cebu, the Spaniards failed to subjugate the Mactan barangay.

In Pilipinas, towns and cities are divided into barangays for effective government. Up to 2,000 persons comprise a barangay and they elect their barangay chief, counselors and other officials who administer a budget and govern the affairs of the barangay. Politics that seem to run in the blood of Pilipinos make the barangays very vigorous centers for government activity and for people making important decisions. Even the youth are active in barangay programs --- a very positive sign of success of local government initiative.

Before the Spaniards imposed their type of government in the archipelago they later called *Las Islas Filipinas*, the barangays had chiefs called *datus*. When barangays were merged as in the big cluster of barangays called Maynilad at the mouth of the Pasig River, they had Rajah Soliman for a ruler. In the south, in Mindanao, the barangays were gathered into barangay clusters under one ruler, like Sultan Kudarat. For a while, combined barangays repulsed the Spaniards. Some unified barangays also resisted and never surrendered the barangays to American domination.

Throughout Pilipinas, as in the mountain provinces and many other places in Luzon, as in the Bisayas and in Mindanao, people cluster into barangays because of their common needs and shared cultural traits. Slowly but surely, this barangay impulse translates into a force for unifying the whole nation facing global political and economic challenges.

BARANGAY ACTIVITY

Your barangay is your own family. Father, or perhaps mother, is the barangay chief who will conduct an election of up to six counselors and other officers, such as a treasurer and a secretary. Sum up all the amount of monies that your barangay spent last year, then make a budget of the barangay for the coming year.

Give your barangay a name and plan a celebration, like the wedding anniversary of the chief of your barangay.

SOURCES:
Miguel A. Bernard, S.J., 1982, Tradition and Discontinuity: Essays on Philippine History and Culture. Manila: National Bookstore.
William Henry Scott, 1984, Prehispanic Source Materials for the Study of Philippine History. Quezon City: New Day Publishers.
Filipino Heritage: The Making of a Nation, Alfredo R. Roces. Ed., 1977. Manila: Lahing Pilipino Publishing, Inc.

Bisayans proudly claim the Lapulapu heritage of valor. In many places in the Bisayas, guitars and other stringed instruments are part of community life. The manufacture of guitars is one of the signs of Bisayan artistic and cultural viability.

B is also for *Bisayas*

Bahay man ay palasyo kung ang nakatira ay kuwago, mabuti pa ang isang kubo na ang nakatira ay tao.

The **Bisayas** is an archipelago within the Pilipinas archipelago comprised of the major islands Panay, Guimaras, Negros, Siquijor, Cebu, Bohol, Leyte, and Samar.

The explorer Ferdinand Magellan and his sailors first landed on an east coast islet where they held the first liturgical mass and claimed the islands in the name of Spain. The Spaniards succeeded in winning the Bisayans under Rajah Humabon of Cebu who brought his barangays into Christianity, opening the way for the near-total Catholization of Pilipinas.

Although Cebu had became the center of early Spanish colonization activities, in 1565 Miguel Lopez de Legaspi met resistance by defiant Cebuano Bisayans.

In 1744 in Bohol, Francisco Dagohoy, angered by a Spanish friar who refused his brother a Christian burial, incited more than twenty thousand Bohol Bisayans to challenge the colonizers. Dagohoy's defiant "Republic of Bohol" lasted eighty five years.

The Spaniards discovered Manila and transferred the colony's capital there, but Bisayans continued to serve the colonial government. Bisayans built galleons for the Spaniards. Sailors from Panay, Negros and Cebu are on record to have received the sacrament of confirmation from Fr. Junipero Serra at his mission church in Monterey, California. In 1750, a Bisayan galleon crewman became one of the sailors who jumped ship and established as early as 1565 the "Manilamen" community in the bayous of Louisiana.

The Bisayan language is of the same language family as the Indonesian. The link is traceable to the Shri-Vishaya empire which reached Pilipinas during A.D. 1200-1400. *Vishaya* is a Sanskrit word meaning victory.

As the strong cultural and economic rival of Metro Manila, Cebu City calls attention to the need to decentralize the Pilipinas government which is overconcentrated in the capital. Bisayan immigrants to Mindanao are active articulate partners with native Mindanaoans in demanding that government render equitable distribution of resources throughout the nation. This demand is oftentimes accompanied by violent armed action and threat of secession that cannot be ignored without disastrous effect.

Besides Cebu, other progressive Bisayan cities like Bacolod, Iloilo and Tacloban, as well as other productive business and commercial centers, contribute dramatically to Pilipino national development.

BARANGAY ACTIVITY

Learn a Bisayan song or dance. Check out the sinulog or the ati-atihan. These are grand dances and very meaningful festivals or rituals.

SOURCES:
Folk Culture of Central Visayas, Pacifico Aprieto, Ed. Manila: Ministry of Education, Culture and Sports, 1986.
Greg Macabenta, "Filipino Historical Footprints" San Francisco: Filipinas Magazine, October 1994.

U. S. Commodore John Dewey's flotilla destroyed the Spanish armada commanded by Adm. Montojo in Manila Bay, a defeat that caused Pilipinas to be handed down from one colonialist ruler to another.

C is for *Corregidor*

Corregidor, an islet near the mouth of Manila Bay, symbolizes Pilipino valor. The Spaniards were first to fortify Corregidor as a strategic defense against invaders coming through the bay. Later, Americans also depended on Corregidor as primary defense.

Ironically, in 1898, at the height of the Spanish-American war, the U.S. Navy flotilla commanded by Commodore George Dewey sank the Spanish armada not far from the Corregidor. That defeat eventually forced the Spaniards to turn over Pilipinas to American domination and exploitation at the Treaty of Paris for twenty million dollars only.

Americans in turn developed Corregidor by mounting large guns ready against expected naval invasions. But World War II raged with different war technology and strategy that rendered Corregidor armor useless. Japanese invaders landed far north in unguarded Lingayen and almost without resistance captured Manila. Inadequate though valorous Pilipino and American defenses in Corregidor and Bataan crumbled. In April 1942, thousands of Pilipino and American prisoners of war suffered in the infamous Death March and worse hardship in prison at Camp O'Donell in Tarlac.

However, Corregidor courage was relived in guerrilla resistance throughout the nation, delaying and ultimately frustrating the Japanese in their Asian campaign. In time, American war effort provided Gen. Douglas MacArthur the military muscle to fulfill his promise, "I Shall Return," and, with invaluable Pilipino gallantry, reconquered Pilipinas.

The United States developed in Pilipinas a defense system through the Philippine Army. Another American military creation was the Philippine Scouts which also saw a lot of action during World War II. For internal security, the Philippine Constabulary was formed. The soldiers in these units became the bulwark of defense during the Japanese-American War. Today, many of the Filipino veterans, almost all old and feeble, await full U.S. recognition of their war effort.

Pinoys in the U.S. formed the 1st and 2nd Infantry Regiments of the U.S. Army and these units were also used against the Japanese occupation forces in Pilipinas.

After World War II, the U.S. maintained military bases in Subic Bay in Olongapo, Sangley Point at Cavite, Clark Air Base in Pampanga, and the R & R facility in Camp John Hay in Baguio, all of which reverted to Pilipino control in 1992.

BARANGAY ACTIVITY

Look up the name of General Douglas MacArthur in an encyclopedia. Write a short biodata and draw a picture of the general, with corncob pipe and the cap.

List names of Pilipino veterans of the Japanese-American War who are residing in your area. Find out what kind of veterans benefit they are demanding and what they deserve.

SOURCES:
Moorfield Storey & Marcial P. Lichauco, 1926, The Conquest of the Philippines by the United States, 1898-1925. New York: G. P. Putnam's Sons.
Gregorio F. Zaide, 1984, Philippine History (Updated Edition). MetroManila: National Book Store.

Pilipino superhero Bantugan of the Darangen legend of the Maranaos never fails to save his people or bring them good. Adults told stories of the mighty feats of heroes and heroines in legends and myths to impart right values and guidelines for action to the young.

D is for *Darangen*

Darangen is the Pilipino legend starring superhero Bantugan. It is recited or sung by epic story tellers among the Maranaws in Mindanao. Like comic book hero Superman, Bantugan in the Darangen legend cannot be defeated or killed. His virtues and exploits always benefit his community. Bantugan is fabled (in fact, *Bantugan* means well-known or popular) to be the earliest user of the Pilipino martial arts known today as *Eskrima* or *Arnis*.

In other regions, Pilipinos recite and sing epics and legends about how the world was created, what heroes appeared to defend the people against their enemies, and how happiness and prosperity come to the community. These very old stories define virtues and values which are vehicles for handing down social and spiritual insights to succeeding generations.

Other important epics or legends are the *Indarapatra at Sulayman* of Maguindanaos; *Hinilawod* of Panay; *Ulalim* of Kalinga; *Ibalon* of Bicolanos; *Biag ti Lam-ang* of Ilocanos; *Hudhud* and *Alim*, both of Ifugaos; *Ulahingan* of Manobos; *Tuwaang* of Bagobos; *Parang Sabil* of Tausogs and *Bavayan* of Bukidnons.

Of similar value to community identity are myths, like the Tagalog story of the creation of *Malakas at Maganda* (Strong and Beautiful), the first couple released from their confines in the bamboo by the holy bird *Tigmamanukin*, also known as *Sarimanok*.

Then there are fun stories, like the Bisayan tales about *Juan Pusong*, a funny man like some sort of Bisayan Forrest Gump, forever bungling into triumph, fame and prosperity.

BARANGAY ACTIVITY

Draw your most favorite comic hero and place him in an imagined Pilipinas situation. Give your comic book hero a name? What does your hero accomplish for the people and what are the people's responses to his great heroic acts on their behalf? Practice telling the story to some one in your barangay. Tape it for others to hear, perhaps for your future use.

Pilipinos call the stories of superheroes "old time history" or "stories of the first time" because through them people learn about the beliefs of their ancestors and the values that govern their decisions and actions.

When Christianity was introduced to Pilipinos, the people were forced to abandon these old time stories because missionaries, teachers and priests discouraged the people from clinging on to their past. So, while Pilipinos learned new values from the stories by Spaniards and Americans who occupied Pilipinas, they were deprived of the benefits of traditional community wisdom. New religions teach values that clash with local customs and mores. Today young Pilipinos are caught in the confusion between traditions that are rebuffed and new sets of values which are often worthless.

SOURCES:
Elena Maquiso,1991, Ulahingan: An Epic of Southern Philippines. Dumaguete City: Silliman University Press.
F. Landa Jocano, 1975, Philippine Prehistory. Quezon City: Philippine Center for Advanced Studies, University of the Philippines.

This sixteenth century engraving depicts priest, king, and explorer in conference on the subject of their new colony shown on the map. The galleon was the chief means of transportation of the explorers turned *conquistadores*.

E is for *España*

España is Spain which, as an old world power, colonized Pilipinas from 1527 to 1898, about the same time that it also colonized Mexico. España shaped the lives and destiny of Pilipinos during those years of domination and control.

The Spaniards named the colony *Las Islas Filipinas* in honor of the child king of Spain, Felipe II. *Español* or Spanish was the language

Because of more than three centuries of cultural influence, the imprint of España on Pilipino culture will remain forever. People and places have Spanish names. Food with Spanish names dominate Pilipino cuisine and diet.

The Roman Catholic Church came with the Spanish conquest and was so influential that even to this day, more than 83% of Pilipinos consider themselves Roman Catholic.

Español, the Spanish language, was learned by some Pilipinos, but really mastered by few. The language was used exclusively in the big towns and cities for official business, like government or church records. A pidgin *Español* called *Chabacano* is considered a vernacular, spoken by Pilipinos in Cavite and Zamboanga.

Even today, *Español*, along with English and Pilipino, is considered a language for doing official business, although it's use is remaining as a mark of antiquity.

Some Pilipino families gained much advantage from attaching themselves to the Spanish elite and are very proud of being *Español* even in name only. Having *Español* name is still a status symbol in Pilipinas today. The contradiction is that, for many Pilipinos, anything non-native is a status symbol. Pilipinos are always fascinated by things that are imported, particularly from America or Europe.

Pilipinos who insist on putting on foreign airs and living a non-native life style are said to have a "colonial mentality." This mind set, many say, explains the slow national progress.

spoken by the conquerors so that a significant number of Pilipinos, particularly the *ilustrados* or the privileged elite in the cities and big towns, spoke the foreign language. Jose Rizal, as example of the few who mastered the language, wrote his novels in *Español*, until recently, one of the official languages in Pilipinas.

BARANGAY ACTIVITY

Make a list of names of people you know are in Español. Make another list Pilipino things with names of Spanish origin, like sibuyas, bintana, lamesa, kotse, kabayo, pantalon, adobo, etc.

But because *España* governed the colony poorly in many respects, Spanish officials were hated for their cruelty and ineptness. Spanish clergy were guilty of tyranny and abuse. Pilipinos slowly understood oppression and the need to fight for freedom. When they had the chance they revolted and began to shake the yoke of *España* off the people's back.

SOURCE:
John Leddy Phelan, 1959, Hispanization of the Philippines. Madison: University of Wisconsin Press.

At the *Santacruzan*, the most popular persons in the community enact personalities like the Boy King Constantine with his very influential mother, Helena. Pilipinos love *pistahan* of all sorts.

F is for *Flores de Mayo*

Sa maliit na dampa nagmumula ang dakila., samantalang ang kasipagan ay kapatid ng kayamanan.

Flores de Mayo, literally "flowers of May," is one of the multifarious, colorful community *pistahan* or celebrations in Pilipinas, much like cherry blossom festivals are memorable to people in Washington DC or Japan in spring. But because Pilipinas has no marked seasons and flowers bloom the whole year round, the emphasis of *Flores de Mayo* is really in religion.

Oral traditions among Pilipino indigenous communities reveal a strong belief in the spirit world dominated by beings like *Bathala*, who not only created the universe but continues to compassionately care for creation. Even before the Spaniards came, the people observed cycles of celebrations as expressions of their belief in superhuman forces influencing nature and people. Community celebrations easily translated into the fiesta or *pista* centered around the church observance to honor a saint.

Santacruzan is the *pistahan* of the legend about the cross of Jesus Christ given to the Roman ruler Constantine as a sign of success in conquest. By combining the missionary outreach of the church and the military exploits of the Roman army, Constantine ruled the Holy Roman Empire--- church and empire in political merger.

Flores de Mayo and s*antacruzan* literally make the community bloom, especially in barangays in MetroManila where movie actors and actresses dress up for the roles enacting legendary personalities in religious pageantry to everyone's delight or sanctification.

In *pistahan* like the *santacruzan*, Christian rituals blend with old community practices. In the *sinulog* of Cebu and the *ati-atihan* of Aklan, dancers costumed as heathen natives, in some places numbering hundreds, take over the city streets to honor the Santo Niño.

Unfortunately, many Pilipinos spend for *pistahan* far beyond their means, borrow money for a big blow out in honor of their patron saint, only to end up having to pay the debt the rest of the year or longer.

Another undesirable thing is when selfish people, even community leaders, see the *pista* merely as another fund-raiser. It would be desirable if the *pista* spirit, bolstered by the *bayanihan* virtue, brings people together and enriches them spiritually to increase their will to work cooperatively. Engaging as a united community in projects that, as example, promote national health or economic productivity would be a commendable way of employing the noble *pista* spirit.

BARANGAY ACTIVITY

Get a picture of people celebrating a Pilipino festival. Find out who the patron saint is. Draw the basic costume used. Wouldn't that be an idea for your next costume party or perhaps for a show-and-tell in school?

SOURCE:
T. Valentino Sitoy Jr., 1985, A History of Christianity in the Philippines: The Initial Encounter, Vol. 1. Quezon City: New Day Publishers.

Attempts by the Spaniards to frustrate the secularization movement of Pilipino priests by executing Gomes, Burgos and Zamora backfired. The martyrs' deaths instead hastened the revolution and also triggered the formation of *La Iglesia Catolica Filipina Independiente*, the Philippine Independent (non-Roman) Catholic Church.

G is for *GomBurZa*

GomBurZa is a Katipunan password, short for Gomes, Burgos and Zamora --- Pilipino priests who were garrotted to death at Bagumbayan on February 17, 1892 upon orders by then Governor Rafael de Izquierdo, allegedly for their participation in a laborers mutiny at Fort San Felipe, Cavite.

The truth was that these Filipino priests were championing the secularization movement, insisting that Pilipino priests deserved the status Spaniards tended to monopolize for themselves. Fr. Mariano Gomes organized his diocese to raise funds to support the secularization movement. Fr. Jose Burgos wrote *"Manifesto a la Noble Nacion Española"* to denounce Spanish friars who were prejudicial against Pilipino priests. Fr Jacinto Zamora celebrated a high mass contrary to church rule that Pilipino priests could merely minister as assistants to Spanish priests.

Gov. Izquierdo ordered Archbishop Meliton Martinez to defrock the priests but he refused because he knew the Pilipino priests were innocent. Gov. Izquierdo went ahead and set the execution of the three priests. **GomBurZa** were garroted at Bagumbayan (now Luneta Park) where Jose Rizal himself would be executed by a firing squad several years later.

The **GomBurZa** martyrdom inspired Jose Rizal to write his novels, fanning the flames of rebellion, inspiring valor and giving Pilipinos firm resolve for revolution and, ultimately, for free and independent nationhood.

Clergy in the Roman Catholic Church who were supposed to champion justice, instead perpetrated the injustices against Pilipinos for whom they had low regard. Despite Church policy, many Spanish friars refused to grant dignity and worth to Pilipino priests as peers. This discriminatory practice became a major factor in fomenting Pilipino anger against Spanish domination and control.

The Pilipino revolution against Spain was directed at the unjust and exploitative friars many of whom were overly authoritative. There were times when the Archbishop was more abusive than the governor.

The Philippine Independent Church, headed by Fr. Gregorio Aglipay, resulted from Pilipino revulsion of the attitude and behavior of Spanish friars.

The Roman Catholic Church in Pilipinas remains the greatest national influence and dictates the people's thinking on issues, like population control which is considered to be a single powerful factor in national progress ... or regress.

BARANGAY ACTIVITY

Make a list of Pilipino heroes and heroines. Be sure you have at least one for each of the Spanish colonization, the American colonization, and the modern periods.

SOURCES

Jose Rizal, 1886 & 1891, (Translated by Jorge Bocobo, 1956 & 1957) Noli Me Tangere & El Filibusterismo. Quezon City: R. Martinez & Sons.

John Foreman, 1906, The Philippine Islands. New York: Charles Scribner's Sons.

Gabriela Silang continued the rebellion in the Ilocos region that was started by her husband, Diego Silang. Although she too was executed, her heroism has become the inspiration for the effective organized crusade for women's causes.

G is also for *Gabriela*

Gabriela is Gabriela Silang, the heroine. It is also the name of the Pilipino organization which champions causes affecting Pilipino women.

Gabriela Silang fought alongside her husband Diego Silang against the abusive Spanish officials. They were supported by Pilipinos in Ilocandia, Pangasinan and the Cagayan Valley but he was betrayed by other Pilipinos and assassinated by a mestizo.

In 1763 Gabriela continued her husband's struggle and became the first Pilipina revolutionary leader. She was defeated by Spanish soldiers because of the betrayal, again, by other Pilipinos. She was hanged.

The record of national heroines includes: the beautiful Purmassuri of Sulu who assisted the moro chiefs to defeat the Spaniards in Sulu; the very wise Princess Urduja of Pangasinan; Teodora Alonzo, the mother and mentor of the national hero Jose Rizal; Melchora Aquino or Tandang Sora, who fed and cared for Katipuneros at their battles against the Spaniards; the only woman Katipunan general Agueda Kahabagan of Batangas; and Trinidad Tecson who procured arms for Gen. Emilio Aguinaldo's war against the Spaniards and, later on, the Americans.

Pilipinos remember Cory Aquino, widow of Ninoy Aquino who was murdered in 1983. Cory became the rallying point of the People's Power revolution that, with thousands of unarmed civilian Pilipinos confronting the armed forces on February 22, 1986, toppled the dictatorial rule of Ferdinand Marcos. She became the seventh and first woman president of Pilipinas.

It's tragic that at the other extreme of the record of achievement, many Pilipino women were abused as comfort women by the Japanese occupation army and, later on, as prostitutes and mothers without husbands by the Americans. Even as this is written today, hundreds of Pilipino women are being exported to other nations as domestics and entertainers, still suffering abuse far away from home, often with no one to protect them or fight for their rights. Sex tourism is a scandalous Pilipino hallmark, presumed necessary like selling rice and *patis* fish sauce.

How can there be justice for Pilipino women somehow, someday ---- soon?

With momentum gained in history and since the right of suffrage bill of December 7, 1933, women movements in Pilipinas have grown strong. Coalescing under the umbrella organization called GABRIELA and other women movements, Pilipino women are making the difference in national progress.

BARANGAY ACTIVITY.

Let mother be the barangay chief to guide the barangay to act on a very important issue. If she is already in charge, deal with toughest issue faced by your barangay. Challenge the barangay to make the toughest decision on behalf of women.

SOURCES:
Maria Odulio de Guzman, 1967, The Filipino Heroes. Manila: National Book Store.
Penny Azarcon de la Cruz, 1994, In the Name of the Mother. San Francisco: Filipinas Magazine, March 1994.

Rajah Humabon welcomed the unique challenge of governing his barangay while under foreign control, thus pioneering the kind of leadership which is ecumenical and international, consonant with modern global mindedness.

H is for *Humabon*

Rajah **Humabon** was the ruler of Cebu when Magellan came in 1521. The title *rajah* indicates that Humabon was well respected and had a great following. Humabon and Magellan celebrated their friendship with a blood compact, a ritual where two people drank of each other's blood and became virtual brothers pledged to support one another.

Magellan wanted to impress his new blood brother by offering his seasoned soldiers to fight datu Lapulapu of Barangay Bulaia in Mactan island. Lapulapu and his men proved to be the better fighters. They killed Magellan and drove the rest of the Spaniards and their Cebuano cohorts back to Cebu.

By respecting Humabon's station, the Spaniards gained Cebuano support. Humabon and the people of Cebu also benefitted from the goodwill that developed.

When Miguel Lopez de Legaspi brought fresh conquistadores to occupy Cebu forty years later, the Cebuanos led by Rajah Tupas were unfriendly. The Cebuanos burned their city and fled to the hills.

The Spaniards meantime had discovered Maynilad or Manila in Luzon. In 1571 Martin de Goiti defeated Rajah Soliman in the battle of Maynilad which the Spaniards made the new capital of the colony.

BARANGAY ACTIVITY

Talk about the Pilipino blood compact. Make a list of ways by which agreements, contracts, alliances, etc. are sealed today. Talk about your own experience of a contract or agreement with someone and how you formalized it.

SOURCES:

Gregorio Zaide, 1984, Philippine History. MetroManila: National Book Store.

Maria Odulio de Guzman, 1967, The Filipino Heroes (*Ang Mga Bayaning Pilipino*). Metro Manila: National Book Store, Inc.

Rajah Humabon readily accepted the Spanish conquistadores. Lapulapu resisted the coming of the Spaniards and drove them back when they invaded his barangay. Leaders like Humabon who embrace foreign ways readily promote change and help people discover new ways of doing things. Cebu became the focus of Catholization, symbolized by the popularity of the Sto. Niño which legend says was given by Magellan to the people of Cebu.

On the other hand, the attitude of submitting to foreign domination is regarded as treason. During World War II, many Pilipinos were denounced as collaborators for taking part in local government under the command of the Japanese.

During the American occupation of Pilipinas, many Pilipino leaders allowed Americans to influence national thinking. For example, Jose Rizal was made the national hero as dictated, they say, by the Americans because Rizal advocated nonviolent changes. In contrast, Andres Bonifacio organized the Katipunan and led the nation in armed revolt against the colonizer. There are Pilipinos who believe that only Bonifacio's kind of nationalism will move the nation to progress.

I is for *Intramuros*

Intramuros, "inside wall," is the stone enclosure built at the height of the Spanish occupation to protect Manila. The walled city had fifty four blocks for government offices, residences, churches and the high places where the rich and famous would gather. Earlier, when it was ruled by Rajah Soliman, Manila was already a palisaded area, protected from invaders, but open to Japanese, Arabian, Chinese and Malayan traders.

When they conquered Manila, the Spaniards built Fort Santiago on the piece of land where the Pasig River flowed into Manila Bay. Later they decided to fortify the whole city and employed Chinese and Pilipino labor to build the four kilometers of walls with moats, a pentagon with seven gates. Only Spaniards were allowed to stay inside Intramuros.

All important decisions about the fate of Pilipinos were made inside Intramuros. However, the British defeated Spaniards in battle and occupied Manila in 1762. After the British withdrew two years later, the image of the not-so-invincible Spaniard encouraged Pilipino protests and rebellions which eventually escalated into the Revolution of 1896.

Outside the wall, the Spaniards encouraged the growth of the Parian marketplace which was dominated by resident Chinese merchants. The Chinese had been prominent in commerce with Pilipinos long before the Spaniards came. As non-Spaniards excluded from the inner city, the Chinese developed the unique relations with the natives. Meztizos or half-breeds, even Chinese meztizos, like Rizal (*Dee San?*), with their

European enlightenment, began to positively assume the status of Pilipino---perhaps the first time someone said *"Ako'y Pilipino!"* with pride.

Insignificant little Chinatown or Parian has in-grown to become the very vital beat of all Pilipino commerce. Meantime, Intramuros is a mute though profound witness to history.

Using Intramuros, the Spaniards segregated themselves from the Pilipinos, Chinese and other inhabitants of old Manila. The Intramuros mentality continues among a large number of rich and not-so-rich Pilipinos who haughtily build high, expensive and ugly walls around their houses. As someone observed, "The rich people live in their own very beautiful slums."

The Intramuros mentality is a commentary on Pilipino penchant for creating factional gaps, like between the ultra-rich and the ultra-poor. Much money is wasted on putting up appearances of progress, an act Pilipinos call *palabas*, meaning---just for show.

BARANGAY ACTIVITY

Make a list of the ways people protect their homes. Include methods like barking dogs and quacking geese, as well as electronic and other forms of so-called safety and security devices. Estimate the cost of building such security device.

SOURCES:
Mariel N. Francisco & Fe Maria C. Arriola, 1987, The History of the Burgis. Quezon City: GCF Books.
The Student's Philippine Almanac. Quezon City: Children's Communication Center, 1991.

The Jeepney and the Moon Buggy are both products of Pilipino inventiveness and resourcefulness. So what's keeping Pilipinas from being fully industrialized so that Pilipinos can build cars and trucks instead of just importing parts and putting them together in "beauty parlor industries?"

J is for *Jeepney*

The **jeepney** is Pilipino---economical, practical and versatile. The first *jeepneys* were built from scrapped World War II army jeeps. Pilipino ingenuity converted scrap into a practical, delightful vehicle which serves the primary transportation needs of communities all over the nation. From eight to twelve persons are accommodated in this locally-adapted minibus. With bountiful frills and trims complementing loud stereo music, the *jeepney* is a fiesta on wheels.

A close cousin of the *jeepney* is the moon buggy or the Land Rover which was used by the Apollo XV lunar mission in 1971. It was invented by Eduardo C. San Juan, a graduate of Mapua Institute of Technology. Ripley's Believe It Or Not dubs San Juan "The Space Junkman." As a designer for Lockheed Missiles and Space Corporation and, like his *kababayan jeepney* maker, San Juan made the moon buggy prototype from scraps. The U.S. National Aeronautics and Space Administration (NASA) and the U.S. Strategic Defense Initiative or Star Wars use San Juan's inventiveness for several of their out-of-this world projects.

Environmental considerations and rivalry from bus owners force the debate that may result in the *jeepney* being banned because detractors claim that *jeepneys* crowd the streets and pollute the city. Will Pilipino ingenuity and practicality prevail by their being able to produce vehicles that do not pollute the environment? What will happen to the *jeepney*?

BARANGAY ACTIVITY

Compare the jeepney with the electric golf cart. Imagine that you are an important government official in charge of improving the jeepney so that it will become be more fitting to Metro Manila. Make suggestions for changes on the jeepney.

SOURCE:
Filipino Heritage: The Making of a Nation. Manila: Lahing Pilipino Publishing Inc., 1977.

The Manila driver, like most Pilipino workers, face many problems every day: earning enough to meet the needs of the family, ensuring the future with health and education for all, and just trying to be a healthy, happy human being.

Pilipino workers in Manila are among the most impoverished in the nation. They'll do anything to make their family happy. Poor workers and farmers suffer the same hopelessness in the face of day-to-day hardship and weariness.

If Pilipinas is to truly progress, the government must have a program to provide opportunity for workers to progress and contribute to national development. Today, *jeepney* drivers and other workers in Manila streets are paupers in their own homeland. A few are ultrarich and uncaring. How can Pilipino ingenuity be harnessed with capital held by the privileged few so that Pilipinos can manufacture cars? Who is holding off the major industrialization of the country?

From Jose Rizal, the Katipunan gained the initial impulse for the Revolution. In turn Andres Bonifacio gave the Katipunan muscle and fighting spirit. Apolinario Mabini provided the intellectual framework that transformed the Revolution so that Emilio Aguinaldo could give it actual form by declaring Pilipino national independence and creating the First Republic.

K is for *Katipunan*

Katipunan means *association*. Katipunan is also the short name for the revolutionary organization that broke Spanish control over Pilipinas.

In 1880, Pilipinos studying in Europe formed *Comité de Propaganda*. Later they organized *Los Indios Bravos* and distributed the newspaper, *La Solidaridád*, for their Propaganda Movement.

Jose Rizal came home from his studies in Europe and formed *La Liga Filipina* intent on securing peaceful reforms from the Spanish government. However, revolutionaries like Andres Bonifacio, preferred the complete overthrow of Spain, so on July 7, 1892 Pilipinos formed the *Kagalanggalang Kataastaasang Katipunan ng mga Anak ng Bayan (KKK)*, Most Exalted, Most Honored Association of the Nation's Children. Most of those who joined the Katipunan were workers, like their leader Andres Bonifacio. They signed membership in the Katipunan with their own blood.

On August 21, 1896 Andres Bonifacio summoned *katipuneros* to Balintawak in Rizal province with the cry *"Mabuhay ang Pilipinas!"* The next day they proceeded to Pugadlawin where they were joined by more than 500 *katipuneros* armed with spears and bolos. Defying authorities, they tore their *cedulas* or certificate of citizenship and proceeded to wage war against Spain to win freedom for Pilipinas.

Before the Katipunan was formed, some Pilipinos tried to get the colony, *Las Islas Filipinas,* accepted as a province of Spain, thinking that by securing reforms, such as a stronger government to replace the control of the islands by friars, Pilipinos would get better treatment from the Spaniards. However, the overwhelming drive to be an independent nation gave inspiration and vision to the Katipunan. Eventually, the people gained power and developed strategy to defeat the Spanish colonizers.

During the American occupation of Pilipinas, the Katipunan was outlawed. Driven underground and borrowing masonic organizational forms, a faction called *Caballeros de Dimasalang* was organized in 1906 by Patricio Belen. The *Caballeros de Dimasalang*, child of the Katipunan and freemasonry, aimed at continuing the fight for independence in the United States.

Perhaps today, one more upbeat Katipunan is needed to galvanize Pilipinos into unity against the enemies of the time.

BARANGAY ACTIVITY

Write a mission statement for your barangay, complete with goals and objectives. What could replace signing with blood as a way of celebrating participation in barangay decision and activity?

SOURCES:

Santiago V. Alvarez, 1992, The Katipunan and the Revolution: Memoirs of a General. Manila: Ateneo de Manila University Press.

Melchizedek Solis, 1985, "Barangay: A Filipino American Experience" Unpublished dissertation. San Anselmo: San Francisco Theological Seminary.

Francis St. Clair, 1902, The Katipunan: The Rise and Fall of the Filipino Commune. Manila: TIP "Amigos del Pais," Palacio 258.

This detail of the mural by Manuel Baldemor of Paete, Laguna shows the many facets of the jewel that is Luzon, particularly Southern Tagalog where the artist lives. Depicted are places to see, like Taal Volcano lake, Laguna de Bay, Antipolo and others. Then there are the festivals and religious celebrations, like the *pahiyas*, the *Moriones* and the *karakol*. Crafts by all types of artisans are also shown. And then there are the heroes highlighted by the forms of Jose Rizal, Manuel Luis Quezon, Emilio Aguinaldo and Apolinario Mabini. There is so much history and culture in this area it is called, *Duyan ng Magiting* (the Cradle of Heroes).

L is for *Luzon*

Ang kapalaran di ko man hanapin,
kusang dudulog, lalapit kung talagang akin.

Luzon is the largest island in Pilipinas. The second largest is Mindanao.

Among Luzon's many attractions are:
(1) The rice terraces, one of the world's original engineering and social wonder in the northern mountain provinces; (2) The Hundred Islands, a tourist-drawing network of islets that speckle the seacoast of Pangasinan; (3) The Central Plains of Luzon, the erstwhile Rice Granary of Pilipinas, comprised of the provinces of Bulacan, Nueva Ecija, Pampanga, Pangasinan and Tarlac; (4) The Subic Bay Freeport project, formerly the U.S. Navy base; (5) Laguna de Bay with its myriads of example of Tagalog community life; (6) Manila, many cities tied together into an extensive kaleidoscope of inexhaustible sights and experiences; and (7) the beautiful near-perfect-coned Mayon volcano in Albay.

A surge to watch is CALABARZON--- the combined provinces of Cavite, Laguna, Batangas, Rizal and Quezon with a new economic development program---presaging, as many claim, the awakening and rise of the next economic dragon of Asia.

Quezon City, the capital of Pilipinas, is part of Metro Manila. Many major government buildings, including the University of the Philippines, are located in Quezon City.

Luzon's natural and people resources are crucial to national development. The addition of forces afforded by the concentration of government and NGO (non-governmental organization) programs ---- make Luzon, particularly Manila, foremost as a factor for national progress.

One problem with concentrating power and influence in the capital is the antagonism and hostility of Pilipinos in areas like Mindanao who clamor for deserved attention. Of course, this is the phenomenon of most third world nations where the metropolitan city monopolizes the advantages of national development.

The greater threat to Pilipino development is the tendency of Pilipinos in power to sell priceless patrimony to foreigners for the mess of get-rich-quick pottage. Residents seem impotent in resisting foreign money. Seashores and foothills become resorts, whole valleys and mountain sides are bulldozed for golf courses. Businessmen politicians grow richer, Pilipinas becomes poorer.

Is it a wound which will never heal? Isn't there a Pilipino leader who can rise to teach by personal example how Pilipinos can love the land entrusted by our ancestors for Pilipino children's children?

BARANGAY ACTIVITY

Look at your map of Pilipinas one more time and see how easily the archipelago is divided into Luzon, Bisayas and Mindanao. Ask an elder in your barangay to locate the places in Luzon mentioned in this section.

SOURCES:
Duyan ng Magiting, Pacifico Aprieto, Ed. Quezon City: Instructional Materials Corp. 1989.
Renato Constantino, 1975, The Philippines: A Past Revisited. Quezon City: Renato Constantino.

M is for *MetroManila*

MetroManila is the governing region that includes urban sections of Manila, Quezon City, Makati, Caloocan, Tondo, Mandaluyong, Pasig, Pasay and Parañaque. MetroManila extends north to the industrialized areas of Valenzuela, Bulacan, down south to affluent Muntinlupa City, and eastward to Marikina's mix of homes and factories. Westward is Manila Bay, bustling with sea commerce.

Manila is the metropolis of more than seven million people and growing. During workdays executives and employees pour out from vehicles too numerous for the limited streets and fill skyscrapers that lift their crowns boldly up into the city sky. Right beside these facades of grandeur, the neglected poor waste their lives away in *barong-barongs* or hovels mired in the fetid, clogged edges of esteros, unused waterways turned into garbage dump.

In mid-fifteenth century, the Spaniards took over the rather large barangay at the mouth of the Pasig river called Maynilad. Through musket and missal, Spanish rulers and priests pressed on Pilipinos the Castilian mindset and life-style. Spain ushered Pilipinas to the new world--- Manila was the gateway.

Propped and prodded by foreign loans, Manila and some portion of Pilipinas jet into modernity, marked by mushrooming malls, cathedrals of the god of consumerism .

In Quezon City, the official capital of Pilipinas, are major commercial and government centers, including the legislature or *Batasang Bayan* and many schools, like the University of the Philippines. Old Manila, just like historic Las Piñas with the world's only bamboo organ, tries vainly to retain some bygone-era charm despite decay, despite modernization.

Fascinating Metro Manila is also the visual and aural evidence of the ugly aspect of urbanization --- congested, polluted and crime-ridden. During rush hours, especially if rain causes street flooding ---- parts of the city are choked by traffic and come to a virtual standstill. Seriously limited energy means brownouts/blackouts. At summer time, water bearers line up at water mains illegally tapped because the metropolis is always short of water.

Poverty, misery and despair squat side by side with glitter, glamour and glee. A rich few flaunt money but miserable many lack the means for even the simplest existence. How is this inequity to be cured?

Pilipinas has an enormous debt to lending institutions controlled by the United States. At what sacrifice can Pilipinas be relieved from such a debt burden? What kind of lenders allow the scandalous size of such a debt in the first place?

BARANGAY ACTIVITY
Locate Manila in your map and trace the Pasig river that runs through Metro Manila, naming the places along its way.

SOURCE:
The Philippines: A Manifold Land. MetroManila: Department of Tourism, Philippines, 1993.

Sultan Kudarat was the staunch defender of Pilipino freedom. Both Spanish and American invaders could not penetrate the defense the Mindanaoans put up against the foreign invaders. In frustration, the American occupation created a separate government for Mindanao---a troubled, still-unsettled cleavage.

M is also for *Mindanao*

Mindanao is the second largest island in Pilipinas. Its majestic Mount Apo, 3,148 meters in Davao, followed close by Mt. Kitanglad, 2,380 meters, in Bukidnon, are the nation's highest mountain peaks. Mindanao provides the lone hope of enduring habitat for the Pilipino eagle, *haribon* (from *haring ibon*-King Bird). With a wingspread of about eight feet it is one of the world's largest airborne creatures and has replaced the *maya* as the national bird of Pilipinas.

Mindanao is home to several indigenous Pilipinos--Mandaya, Manobo, B'laan, Bagobo, T'boli, Mansaka and many tribal communities regarded as *lumads* or aborigines. Socially-advanced and culturally value-rich, these original Pilipinos are gradually gaining recognition for their contribution to authentic Pilipino identity. Developed in yet another significant way are the Maranaos in Lanao and the Maguindanaos in Cotabato; together they comprise the heartland of Muslim Pilipinas, estimated at five million faithfuls, as against sixty million Christian Pilipinos.

Commercially developed cities like Davao, Cagayan de Oro, Malaybalay, Sultan Kudarat and General Santos, through modern communications and technological international exchanges, actively link Mindanao and, therefore, Pilipinas to the rest of the world.

Needing to reverse irresponsible and devastating exploitation of natural resources, Pilipinos can yet make Mindanao fulfill the promise and be the country's food security basket.

Mindanao has been regarded as The Land of Promise, but Mindanao is also a problem --- not just a Muslims-versus-Christians religious conflict. Muslim Pilipinos have joined the complaints chorus by other Mindanaoans who point out that the Pilipinas government seated in Manila neglects Mindanao which encompasses major areas of Mindanao island as well as the islands of Palawan, Basilan, Sulu and Tawi-Tawi. Greater Mindanao, they say, remains a virtual colony of Pilipinas. There is a serious threat of secession by those who want an independent Republic of Mindanao.

Most believe though that there is still time and opportunity to deal with the clamor of the people of Mindanao for the deserved right to self-determination and justice. If their cries are heard, Pilipinas can still unite her children without bloodshed or strife.

Working together, Pilipinos are making Mindanao productive, bringing fulfillment to its prophesy of progress and peace.

BARANGAY ACTIVITY

Get a picture of the <u>haribon</u> or Pilipino eagle. Locate the possible locations of the habitat of this magnificent large bird in the island of Mindanao.

Discuss how the extinction of the Philippine eagle can be stopped?

SOURCES:
Reuben R. Canoy, 1991, Mindanao, The Quest for Independence. Cagayan de Oro City: Mindanao Post Publishing Co.
Phiiippines: A Manifold Land. Metro Manila: Department of Tourism, Philippines, 1993.

40

N is for *Narra*

Narra is one of the most desired Pilipino wood from the *molave* species which include *tindalo*, *dao*, and *ipil*. Furniture made of narra wood is on demand beccause the wood's reddish hue and grain property is considered by woodworkers as one of the best for engraving. *Narra* is preferred to *lauan*, lumber from the species that provide Philippine mahogany commonly used for plywood.

Molave's resiliency is the poet's paradigm for Pilipino. Other treasures from Pilipinas flora and fauna are held as symbols of Pilipino character. There's the tiny, fragrant *sampaguita* flower---its cool beauty relieve the weariness of the tired and worn. Contrast then the ferocious, swift grandeur of *haribon* or Pilipino eagle----eight feet wingtip to wingtip, total fury and total grace. Or take the *tamaraw* of Mindoro, so ferocious and fleet, very few have had the opportunity to observe this magnificent animal. Nature is a link to Pilipino spirituality, as demonstrated by indigenous religiosity of inhabitants of Mt. Banahaw, Laguna.

The forest is a pharmacological treasure trove from which, for thousands of years before modern medicine, healers have derived reliable cure. The culture of cure through herbs and traditional world views in Pilipinas is attracting commercial pharmaceuticals in search of medicine and treatment technique for yet many never-understood illnesses.

Tropical Pilipinas abounds with so many plant and animal species that could yet be sources of eternal wonder and delight to all.

Besides beauty and contentment, *narra* and all forest life are signals of the right of humans and all living things to coexist on this planet.

Forest resources in Pilipinas are rapidly used up because the nation has no effective program of reforestation or conservation. Worsened evermore by greedy and mindless legislators, government officials and forest product marketers who seem unaware of the limits of wood and lumber supply, wanton deforestation and the human encroachment into forest habitations doom Pilipinas. The nation's forests are fast turning into money for the bank books of a privileged few.

Soon there will be no forests, no wood for furniture nor homes. Even more grimly, with the overharvested forest disappear songs of birds and the rustle of animals. When forest life disappear the countdown to human extinction begins.

BARANGAY ACTIVITY

Examine how much wood is used in your home and decide how long do you think the wood supply on the planet can last? List some ways your barangay participate in conservation of natural planet resources?

SOURCES:
Student's Philippine Almanac. Quezon City: Children's Communication Center, 1991.
Vicente Marasigan, S.J., 1985, A Banahaw Guru. Quezon City: Ateneo de Manila University Press.

Olongapo as a lingering inequity will haunt every concerned human being as long as a miserable abandoned Amerasian child and the equally miserable husbandless mother remain ignored by the American father.

O is for *Olongapo*

Olongapo was little known, even to Pilipinos, until Americans built the naval base at nearby Subic Bay. Literally in a few nights, Olongapo leaped into modernity ---nay, into sinfulness! By the time bases closed in 1992, Olongapo had one main street more than a mile long with night clubs and eateries on both sides. The count was more than 3,000 rest-and-recreation establishments. Military bases have wicked edges of flesh trade outside their fences.

Purportedly to show military preparedness for any global conflict, the United States built the bases. Pilipinas government authorities, eager to be on the side of the world power with the bigger punch and purse, ignored sins committed in the base including the worst, which was the exploitation and abuse of Pilipino women. On the other hand, close to 50,000 Pilipinos found good paying jobs in the American enterprise on Pilipino soil, and they were the ones who opposed the closure of the bases.

The United States had gained rights to operate the base as part of the conditions of independence. Through the 1947 Military Bases Agreement, Pilipinos granted United States rights to operate twenty three bases and reservations "rent free" in Pilipinas for one hundred years, until March 2046.

Fifty four years short, in 1992 Pilipinos stopped allowing Americans to operate the bases. Actually, the bases had become unnecessary as Communism had collapsed. Mt. Pinatubo rained ashes of dismay. The United States was going to close the bases anyway.

Commercial rehabilitation began in 1993 with the Subic Bay Freeport, a project promising new jobs to Pilipino workers and a new future to an economically weak Pilipinas. "Olongapo" in the meantime metamorphosed as naughty night spots with brothels and companion services in many cities.

Because of the American bases, thousands of Pilipino women, many very young innocent girls, were lured into the sex trade sanctioned by base authorities, with no objection from Pilipino officials. Hardly any girl in this circumstance escapes becoming a prostitute. Left behind are husbandless mothers and fatherless children, painful reminders of the Pilipino American treaty of mutual defense which was disadvantageous to Pilipinos.

Many AIDS-ridden former prostitutes, along with despised, poverty-grounded Amerasian children with their equally despondent mothers, wait for responses from the U.S. government for consideration and deserved compassionate care.

BARANGAY ACTIVITY

Someone in your barangay is reporting for military duty overseas. Make a list of things to watch for to show respect for the integrity of the people where the base is located.

SOURCES:
Student's Philippine Almanac. Quezon City: Children's Communication Center, 1991.
Raissa Espinosa-Robles, "Subic Conversion: From Swords to Common Shares." San Francisco: Filipinas Magazine, June 1993.

Pinoy Demographic Profile in the U.S.

There are more than 2 million Pinoys in the United States.

There are about 1 million in California alone.

Pilipinos have a higher education level than U.S. averages.

The collective annual income of Pilipinos is $12.7 billion.

Among first generation Asian Americans, 97% of Pilipinos are not U.S.-born.

Average length of stay in the U.S. is 12.1 years, 33% have lived in the U.S. from 0-5 years.

There are more females than males among Pilipinos than among the Indians, Chinese, Korean and Japanese.

The Pilipino household has a total of 2.7 adults and 1.9 children---the largest household size among Asians.

Nearly 41% of Filipinos have two adults employed full-time. There are 3-5 employed Pilipinos per household--- again the highest among Asians.

Nearly 40% of Pilipinos hold professional jobs, 7% are entrepreneurs or business owners and 19.3% hold managerial/administrative/ sales and clerical positions.

Close to 53% of Pilipinos own their own homes.

The average household income among Pilipinos is $45,391.

Pilipinos have one of the highest percentage of high school graduates--- 70% compared to the overall population average which is 66.5%. College graduates top 36% versus the national average of 16%.

Pilipino women graduate from high school and college at a higher rate than men do, compared to women of other Asian groups.

SOURCES

U.S. Census Bureau, 1980

U.S. Bureau of Labor Statistics

Philippine News Market Research '80

WOMEN	49%
AGE	
18-34	34%
35-54	34%
55+	25%
EDUCATION	
College graduate	34%
Some college	28%
High School graduate	14%
AVERAGE STAY IN THE U.S.	
5-10 years	25%
11-20 years	37%
HOUSEHOLD SIZE	
1-2 members	32%
3 or more members	58%
OCCUPATION	
Professional, technical managerial	72%
Administrative support, sales	18%
Other employed	10%
HOUSEHOLD INCOME	
$26,000 to $40,000	50%
$41,000 to $75,000	38%
$76,000 and above	10%

SOURCE: Marketing Help Research, 1991.

PINOYS IN CALIFORNIA COUNTIES	
Northern California	733,113
Southern California	408,149
Total in California	733,113

PINOY POPULATION IN BAY AREA	
San Francisco county	42,652
San Mateo county	44,732
Alameda county	52,535
Contra Costa county	24,663
Santa Clara county	61,517

SOURCE: State Census Data Center

PINOY POPULATION IN 3-COUNTY AREA	
Santa Cruz county	2,447
San Benito county	427
Monterey county	11,497

PERCENTAGE OF ASIAN AMERICANS WHO ARE FOREIGN BORN	
Vietnamese	90.40%
Korean	81.89%
Pilipino	64.70%
Chinese	63.3%
Japanese	28.40%

SOURCE: Asian American Health Forum

PERCENTAGE OF ASIAN AMERICANS LIVING BELOW THE POVERTY LEVEL	
Vietnamese	33.5%
Chinese	13.3%
Korean	12.5%
Filipino	6.9%
Japanese	6.6%

SOURCE: Asian American Health Forum

LARGEST NUMBER OF ASIAN OWNED BUSINESSES ARE IN:

		% FILIPINO OWNED
LA-Long Beach	33,150	21%
Honolulu	21,583	13%
SF-Oakland	18,312	23%
Vallejo-Fairfield Napa	1,093	42%
San Diego	6,053	30%

SOURCE: U.S. Dept. of Commerce Economics & Statistics Administration

P is for *Pinoy*

Kung lantay na bakal ka, sa apoy ka makikilala.

Pinoy is the Pilipino overseas. The word *Pinoy* results from Pilipino custom of showing affection by shortening names like Florentino to *Tinoy* or Balbino to *Binoy*. In places like Daly City or San Francisco, they will remark, "Many Pinoy here."

The earliest Pinoys in America settled in *Manilamen* communities in the bayous of Louisiana as early as 1763. Some Pinoys married Mexicans and started families in Mexico. In Monterey, California, church records of Fr. Junipero Sierra in 1770 indicate a visit by Bisayan galleon sailors receiving the sacrament of confirmation, the first Pinoys in California.

At the start of American colonial rule, Pinoy *pensionados* or government scholars came to the U.S. Sugar cane workers for Hawaii and farm workers for California, many of whom spent time in Alaska as cannery workers, began a stream of Pinoy migration in 1906. Pinoys were imported as "laborers primarily as instruments of production ... cheap, not too intelligent, docile unmarried men." By the end of World War II, the Pinoy count in Hawaii alone was more than 125,000.

With the Immigration Act of 1965, Pilipino professionals with their whole families left for the U.S. constituting the "brain drain." Pinoys are migrating to the U.S. in numbers second only to Mexicans. Four million Pinoys are estimated to be overseas, more than two million in the U.S.

Ugly, dark shadows mar the glittering picture of so-called Pinoy achievement in the U.S. For example, a study of Pinoy college students in the University of California and California State University systems revealed that Pilipino American collegians have the lowest rate of success in earning a degree.

More than one half of Pilipino American high school graduates surveyed in a California county had GPAs of 3.00 or above but a majority of these bright Pinoy youths never finished college.

Why? Young Pinoys are inheriting the world view and life-style of parents who superficially show off success rather than genuinely achieve it. Fancy, expensive cars, contemporary-styled clothes, and houses!

For all the claim to numbers of highly educated professional, why have Filipinos failed to produce a congressman or senator? Is it true, this thing about Pinoys, like crabs in a basket dragging the one at the top back down at the bottom of the heap?

SUGGESTED BARANGAY ACTIVITY

List the cities in the United States with the highest concentration of Pinoys. If your barangay can, list the attempts by Pinoys to run for government office and the results.

SOURCE:

"The Filipino American Community of the 1990s," Brochure of the National Filipino American Council. 455 Broadway, Milbrae, California 94030.

Fred Cordoba, 1983, Filipinos: Forgotten Asian Americans. Dubuque: Kendall/Hunt Publishing Co.

Jennifer Stern, 1989, The Filipino Americans. New York: Chelsea House Publishers.

Vice President Sergio Osmeña

Manuel Quezon and Sergio Osmena started the multi-partisan political style developed at the early attempts at democratic government of Pilipinas. There is need for leadership that will continue the maturation and creativity to meet new challenges, particularly in dealing with foreign interests hiding behind Pilipino dummies expropriating the nation's resources.

Q is for *Quezon*

Quezon is the name of a province in Pilipinas. Quezon City is the nation's capital city. This name honors Manuel Luis Quezon, the first president of Pilipinas even when it was U.S.-linked in the Commonwealth in 1935. With Sergio Osmeña, President Quezon ushered Pilipinas into independence and internationalism.

Manuel Quezon was a revolutionary from Tayabas, renamed Quezon to honor him. He fought in the war against the Spaniards and then against the Americans. When the revolution was quelled by America, Quezon carried on his fight for Pilipino independence and integrity. He crusaded for freedom of Pilipinas declaring "A Pilipinas run like hell by Pilipinos is preferable to a Pilipinas run like heaven by Americans."

As part of the first Philippine American commission in Washington D.C., he persuaded the U.S. Congress to fix the date of the granting of independence to Pilipinas with the Tydings-McDuffie Act of 1934. Quezon insisted on Pilipinos asserting their national identity which resulted, among other nationalistic initiatives, in the adoption of Quezon's dialect, Tagalog, as the base for the Pilipino language.

Although Quezon died while Pilipinas was still fighting the Japanese, he is honored for being the father of modern Pilipinas.

BARANGAY ACTIVITY
Make a list of politicians and the places or things named to honor them for their achievements

Quezon was never alone in the good fight for cultural integrity and independence. Besides Osmeña, there were other outstanding nationalists. One such stalwart was Isabelo de los Reyes who wrote and spoke fearlessly against both Spanish and American oppression. With Fr. Gregorio Aglipay, de los Reyes founded the *Iglesia Catolica Filipina Independiente* (Philippine Catholic Independent Church). Later on he established the first Pilipino labor federation, the *Union Obrera Democratica*.

The other great nationalist was Claro Recto who condemned the continued U.S. imperial influence on Pilipino affairs even after independence. As senator, he spoke against concessions made by Pilipino politicians to Washington like: the Parity Amendment to the Constitution which gave Americans equal rights with Pilipinos to exploit Pilipinas natural resources. He opposed acceptance of U.S. military advisors through the JUSMAG or Joint United States Military Advisory Group and the agreement to allow U.S. military bases on Pilipinas soil rent free for a hundred years.

SOURCES:
Manuel Luis Quezon, 1946, The Good Fight: An Autobiography. New York: D. Appleton-Century, Co.
Miguel A. Bernad, S.J., 1982., Tradition and Discontinuity: Essays on Philippine History and Culture. MetroManila: National Bookstore.
Lewis E. Gleeck , Jr., 1986, The American Governors-General and High Commissioners in the Philippnes. Quezon City: New Day Publishers.

General Emilio Aguinaldo proclaims the independence of Pilipinas
from the balcony of his home in Cavite on June 12, 1898 jump-starting the
Constitutional formation of the Pilipinas republic on September 29, 1899.

R is for *Republic*

Pilipinas is a **republic.**

On June 12, 1898, when Pilipinos had a taste of victory over their Spanish colonizers, Gen. Emilio Aguinaldo declared Pilipinas independent from Spain. On September 29, 1899, through the Malolos Constitution, Pilipinos established *Republika ng Pilipinas*, the first republic in Asia.

That republic was short-lived because the United States colonized Pilipinas and later incorporated the nation into the Commonwealth of 1935. In 1943, Pilipinos under Japanese occupation and control proclaimed independence to form the second Pilipino republic that ended with Japan's defeat in 1945.

Independence and republic status --- third in the series --- was asserted by Pilipinos in 1946, allowing the claim, still pending in American courts, that Pilipinos born before 1946 are U.S. nationals entitled to U.S. citizenship.

A republic with parliamentary style of government resulted with the 1973 changes in the Constitution prompted under martial law providing for a President-Prime Minister.

In effect are three branches of government: the legislative branch called *Batasang Pambansa*; the executive branch under the President; and the judicial branch headed by Supreme Court with descending authority in a three-tiered system of local, regional trial and intermediate appeals courts.

Pilipinas is divided into forty seven provincial governments under the national government. The basic socio-political unit is the barangay with its own elected officials headed by the *Punong barangay*.

Pilipino national viability is gauged by its economy which is weakest in terms of per capita income compared to the economic dragons: US-$13,154, Japan-$9,588, Singapore-$5,290, Hongkong-$4,600, Korea- $1607, Thailand-$800, and Pilipinas-$760.

A contention is that Pilipino democracy styled after that of the United States fails because the citizenry base is not as educated or, as claimed, is mis-educated. As a result, Pilipinos fail to follow with power and wisdom the stride towards economic emancipation, political independence and cultural renascence.

In extreme, there is a loud voice saying that, given the colonial mentality of the people, Pilipinas can not be a free republic because it will never be truly independent from the United States. The republic without moral or spiritual roots in its history and culture can not measure up to the demands of independence.

BARANGAY ACTIVITY
Make a comparative list of advantages between a democratic form of government versus that of a monarchy. Which is preferable?

SOURCES:
Renato Constantino, 1971, The Filipinos in the Philippines and Other Essays. Quezon City: Malaya Books, Inc.
Gregorio F. Zaide, 1984, Philippine History. Manila: National Bookstore.

Native games and folk dances are among the best but dwindling options for recreation by Pilipino youth.

50

S is for *Sabong*

Sabong is cockfighting. Is it curse or blessing ... play or plague?

Many Pilipinos call *sabong* the king of sports because no game is enjoyed by so many and so frequently in practically every locality in the country. *Sabong* is legal in Pilipinas. Although illegal in the U.S. a lot of Pinoys are often involved in and caught at raids of cockfighting.

Sabong pits feisty, specially-trained fighting cocks with sharp metal spurs against each other in a bloody battle to death. One really good cock is reputed to be as costly as a house.

Sabong means heavy betting. Cockfighting days are scheduled as regularly as and in dire competition with church services. Community leaders have seen to the building of cockpit arenas called *sabongan* rather than libraries.

Cockfighting experts are as famous as top government officials and heads of service organization. Some fathers favor fighting cocks more than they do their own children.

While the hopeless battle is being fought to take away Pilipino fascination for bloody chicken fights and gambling, the old native games are being forgotten. Who remembers how to play *patintero, sambunot, sipa, harangang-taga, takip-silim, bakunawa, satong, takyan, luksong-tinik,* or *kawat-kawat*?

American games and sports like track, baseball, basketball and volleyball that are promoted by major commercial corporations provide young players preferable activities that instill values essential to healthy citizenship. In the U.S., library and museum officials ask why Pilipinos or Filipino Americans are not seen as clients in proportion to their number.

Otherwise, *sabong* and its accompanying plague of betting and cruelty to roosters has many disciples. It is easier to convince most Filipino Americans to gather for gambling and parties than to attend a PTA meeting or a cultural educational activity.

Sabong, like most gambling activities, is a serious plague that is wasting away the sinews and spirit of the nation. Gambling flows with Pilipino blood. To live is to bet... *"Pustahan tayo?"* (You wanna bet?)

Civic leaders in schools, churches, and service organizations press for the instilling of more constructive values, but as long as *sabong, mahjongg* and a host of other gambling manias, indulged in the name of recreation, are preferred by the large number of Pilipinos, healthy play shall have but a Chinaman's chance. *"Pustahan tayo?"*

BARANGAY ACTIVITY

Make a sipa ball using plastic strips. Make and kick the takyan, *a washer with shredded paper tail. Make games rules and don't bet. Nanay could make sinigang of fighting cock drumsticks with* malunggay. *Yummy!*

SOURCES:
Angel J. Lansang, 1966, Cockfighting in the Philippines: Our Genuine National Sport. MetroManila: M & L. Licudine Enterprises.
Isaac Cruz, Jr., "Filipino Children's Games." Filipinas Magazine, October 1994.

SI	AY-	POD	BAY	U-	PA-	DAN
NO	KANG	TI-	NA-	GIN-DU-	MAN	
MAY	U-	LANG	MA-	DI	KAS-NAN	
MAY	TA-	KIP	NA-	DI	KAY-NAN	
NO	KANG	TI-	NA-	GIN-DU-	MAN	
GA	SI-	YON	DI	SA	AD-	NGAN
GA	PAG-	TANG-DA-	YON	DI-	MAN	

The above text is in the seven-syllable-seven-line *ambahan* style poetry of the Mangyans of Mindoro. It is written in the Pilipino script characters based on ancient Indian writing which the Mangyans still use today. The love poem above translates ---

You, my friend, dearest of all
Thinking of you makes me sad;
Rivers deep are in between
Forests vast keep us apart.
But thinking of you with love:
As if you are here nearby
Standing, sitting at my side.

Upon arrival in Pilipinas, the Spaniards were surprised that the Pilipinos could read and write. Their style of writing was the Asian script derived from ancient script originating in India. (A. Postma, MANSALAY, Mindoro)

T is for *Taglish*

Taglish, a new word coined from **Tag**-alog and **Eng-lish,** names a trend in Pilipino bilingual conversational language. Colonized people tend to be bilingual. In Spanish times they had *landinos* who spoke in alternating lines of Tagalog and Spanish.

Savor Taglish through this fun song with a built-in Tagalog translation:

One day *isang araw*, I saw *nakita ko*
A bird *isang ibon*, flying *lumilipad*
I shot *binaril ko*, I picked *pinulot ko*
I cooked *niluto ko*, I ate *kinain ko*.

Another amusing example of Taglish is this very original ad on credit cards of a U.S. company aimed at Pinoys ----

"*Walang ibang* calling card *ang mas* unique *pa dito*. *Ito'y* personalized. *Ito'y* convenient. *Ito'y matipid*. *Ito'y* world wide. *Ito'y libre*. *Ito'y* available *sa wikang Tagalog*."

A new Pilipino language is evolving which includes all sounds experienced by Pilipinos from Spanish and American languages, as well as from the major vernaculars. In this macaronic process, the Pilipino language lives and grows.

BARANGAY ACTIVITY

Memorize one of the <u>salawikain</u> that are found on top of the pages of this book. Be sure you know the meaning by talking to someone who understands it. Make up a <u>salawikain</u> in Taglish, if you please. Someday you could win a prize for your creation.

Before Spaniards forced the Roman alphabet on Pilipinos, several indigenous tribes had their language written in *alibata*, a syllabary with three vowel sounds (a, e-i, o-u) and fourteen consonants, like the one used by a Spanish missionary in *Doctrina Christiana*, the very first book which was printed in Spanish with Tagalog translation.

Tagalogs wrote *alibata* on bark or bamboo. Similar to Tagalog *alibata*, the Tagbanwa and the Mangyan also have a syllabary which even today they use in short poems, songs, debt records and love letters. Regrettably, these too shall be buried in the grave of the forgotten.

Linguists and other social scientists will have to comment on the unpredictable twists in the development of the language of Pilipinos. Pilipino (based on the Tagalog dialect) was declared by President Quezon as the *wikang pambansa*. A greater number of Pilipinos from Aparri down to Sulu now speak Pilipino. In each region, however, Pilipino is developing differently due to the influence of vernaculars. Taglish is the Manila deviation. A serious blow to nationalism that is supposed to solidify through one *wikang pambansa* is the penchant for American English, especially on mass media, like radio and TV programs backed by big bucks from multi-national sponsors.

SOURCE:
   F. Landa Jocano, 1975. Philippine Prehistory: An Anthropological Overview of the Beginnings of Filipino Society and Culture. Quezon City: Philippine Center for Advanced Studies.

A couple from the Ulog ritualistically confirm pregnancy of the young woman in order to allow the community to move towards the next step of celebrating marriage in the long-established practice of building family and community.

U is for *Ulog*

Ulog, like planting rice in and building the thousand-year-old terraces, is a long-established practice among Pilipinos of Northern Luzon. Actually, the *ulog* is the communal house where marriageable girls gather and sleep, as marriageable boys stay in another communal house called *ato* and they come to the *ulog* to court the girls with songs rich with meaning and insinuation. The girls, in turn, reply in native verse. All these and attending activities between consenting individuals happen under the watchful eye of the *ulog* head, whose duty is to keep family and community informed of the progress of *ulog* love, particularly those accented by pregnancy. Desired results of this custom are childbearing, family stability and community growth.

This love and marriage practice is also followed as *ebgan* with the Kalinga and as *pangis* with the Tingguian.

There are other lingering love and marriage traditions, such as the *panunuyo* or courtship, where the boy declares his devotion to a girl by doing domestic work, such as fetching water, gathering wood and doing whatever occupation the girl's family is engaged in---for as long as seven years, in some cases!

Pilipino marriage remains a community concern, as where a third party does the courting in the *pamanhikan* where the boy's family "goes up" the house of the girl to ask for her hand in marriage.

Community backing is important in marriage. Broken *ulog* marriages are unknown. When marital problems rise, the community provides solutions to sustain the union in the principle that solid families make solid community or nation.

Many critics, including those presumably speaking for the Christian community, denounce the *ulog* because it is simplistically confused with premarital sex. However, those who blindly despise functional traditions ignore the worsening problems of modern love. Taking on Western forms of dating, premarital sex, abortion and easy separation or divorce, Pilipino marriage today is contaminated by Western value crisis with the resultant breakage of families.

Pilipinas laws do not recognize divorce. Under few, selected circumstances the Roman Catholic Church will sanction the intricate process of annulment of a marriage, most often for anyone who need not worry about money.

The loss of the genuine, constructive concern by the barangay or the community over the welfare of the young in marriage and long-term family life is a sad loss. To enjoy the full blessings of family life, Pilipinos need to learn basic principles of interpersonal and social relations from traditions like the *ulog*.

BARANGAY ACTIVITY

Make a list of the methods boys and girls use these days to win the person they admire or love. A good list might come handy when it's your turn to be involved in courtship designed for eventual marriage.

SOURCES:

The Student's Philippine Almanac. Quezon City: Children's Communiction Center, 1991.

Vic Hurley, 1938, Jungle Patrol: The Story of the Philippine Constabulary. New York: E. P. Dutton & Co. Inc.

V is for *Vinta*

The **vinta** is uniquely the sea craft of Pilipinas archipelago. Fleet and economical, the motorized vintas transport people and goods between the islands, particularly among the Samals and Badjao in Mindanao. The *vinta* is so nimble and quick, it is fabled to elude even the fast Coast Guard cutter, especially at night, when powered by silent sails it negotiates interisland channels only *vinta* sailors can navigate when darkness blinds the inexperienced seafarer.

Long before foreigners came, *vintas* served as sea links between Mindanao and Sulu, Borneo and Indonesia, a cultural oneness based on Malayan culture. Similarly, the bigger *barangay* boat mentioned earlier in this book, is clue to ancient ties of Pilipinos with peoples in these southern lands

During the Spanish conquest, Pilipinos were key persons in the galleons trade which flourished between 1565 to 1815. Pilipinos built ocean-going galleons and ship accessories; they also served as galleon crew. Along the route of the galleon, Pilipino sailors escaped from the brutal galleon masters and adventured in seashores of the gulf of Mexico and into the bayous of Louisiana. In St. Malo, Louisiana Pilipinos became the earliest Asian migrants to the U.S. mainland, settling a few years earlier than the pilgrims at Jamestown.

Runaway or swim-away Pilipino galleon sailors settled in Louisiana and were known as *Manilamen*. In their *Manila village* they introduced the sun-dried shrimp industry.

Today Pilipino seamanship are employed by major shipping companies as seamen or administrators of shipping offices and other seafaring enterprises in many parts of the world. More than that, the domestic sea transport industry is flourishing with locally built inter-island ships supplying fast and efficient services.

The *vinta* is a beautiful representation of the integrity and functionality of Pilipino culture. Unfortunately, the *vinta* and many other excellent cultural symbols are lost in conflicts between Christian and Muslim Pilipinos.

Part of the tragedy is that as Pilipinos modernize and get caught in the materialistic whirlpool, many unknowingly allow traditional cultural values to drift like *vintas* lost in the sea of indifference and hostility. This explains why many Pilipinos know nothing about the *kulintang* musical instrument or the *okil* wood carving art.

Aren't all Pilipinos entitled to claiming the culture of people in Southern Pilipinas as part of their total Pilipino heritage?

BARANGAY ACTIVITY
Hold a vinta *drawing contest . Give prizes to the most colorful* vinta *drawings. List other tourist attractions in the Pilipinas.*

SOURCES:
Vic Hurley, 1937, The Swish of the Kris: The Story of the Moros. New York: E. P. Dutton & Co., Inc.
Fred Cordova, 1983, Filipinos: Forgotten Asian Americans. Dubuque, Iowa: Kendall/ Hunt Publishing Co.

Stages in the development of the *watawat ng Pilipinas*

1892   First Pilipino flag

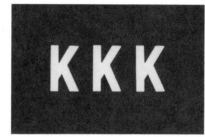

1892   Katipunan war standard

1892   Alternate war standard.

1893   Flag of Gen. Mariano Llanera

1894   Flag of Andres Bonifacio

1895   Flag of Gen.Pio del Pilar

1896   Flag of Gen.Emilio Aguinaldo

1897   Second Pilipino flag

1898   Present flag of Pilipinas

58

W is for *Watawat*

Watawat is the Pilipino word for flag.

The Pilipino flag today was developed from earlier Katipunan versions. Gen. Emilio Aguinaldo ordered one made by Marcela Agoncillo with the help of her daughter, Lorenza, and Delfina Herbora de Natividad. That flag was flown when the first Pilipino Republic was proclaimed at Cavite on June 12, 1898 to signal Pilipino victory over Spain.

Also for the first time the music for the *Pambansang Awit* or national anthem composed by Julian Felipe was played by a band and heard publicly. Jose Palma, much later, wrote the lyrics now sung to the music.

However, when America colonized Pilipinas, the Pilipino flag was hoisted down and, only much later on, allowed to fly side by side with the American flag. Pilipinos were a people under two flags, singing two national anthems, until July 4, 1946 when the American flag was hoisted down permanently. Then Pilipinos had but one flag, one freedom hymn.

On March 25, 1936 President Manuel Quezon ordered the standardization of the Pilipino flag, using the red, white and blue with the yellow sun and stars.

The thought of including symbols for Mindanao or other unincorporated elements of Pilipino life and experience crops up again and again; each time a controversy is stirred. The more inclusive symbol is desired of course, but how readily can change be implemented?

The *watawat na Pilipino* (Pilipino flag) and the *pambansang awit* (national anthem), like the *wikang pambansa* (national language), have been factors for unifying of Pilipinos to a considerable degree. However, there are still chasms of division and regional rivalry that need to be bridged.

BARANGAY ACTIVITY

Make a Pilipino flag, even of paper or vinyl, if you have no cloth. Or buy a Pilipino flag and display it in your room being sure that you know the rules of displaying a flag properly.

SOURCES:
   Filipino Heritage: The Making of a Nation Manila: Lahing Pilipino Publishing Inc., 1977.
   The Students Almanac. Quezon City: Children's Communication Center, 1991.

Flags and other forms of national heraldry unify people, particularly in times of conflict or crisis. It is easy to hear people decry the lack of unity of Pilipinos. Interregional rivalry and, worse, socioeconomic conflicts, as between Christian and non-Christian Pilipinos, discourage the fostering of unity.

What can truly unify Pilipinos?   Is it possible to go back to precolonial times and discover some history and literature or folk culture that could call all Pilipinos to rally together as a unified people?

Or will the economic challenge --- the vision of becoming yet another Asian economic dragon --- be forceful enough to make Pilipinos forget differences and harmoniously pull together to achieve the national agenda of prosperity and progress?

X is for *Ximenez*

Fray Alonso Ximenez was a Dominican friar in Manila. On June 24, 1590, after barely twenty years of Spanish colonization of Pilipinas, he signed a letter urging King Philip of Spain to wage a "just war" against the Negritos and Zambals, blaming them for attacks and robberies because "they are a race who never keep any promise." Other friars also wrote a similar letter urging to the king of Spain "to protect the Tagalogs, Pampangueños, Pangasinan and Ilocanos who are paying tribute."

Fr. Ximenez is typical of the colonizers resorting to divide-and-conquer tactics to split their enemies into infighting factions. Also this colonial approach to control suggested the technique of hamletization, the method of corralling suspected natives into camps where they could be watched or wiped out, when necessary.

Oddly though, the Spaniards were not able to quell all rebelling Pilipinos, much less those in the Mountain provinces or in Mindanao. Americans used more subtle techniques of subjugation. Divisions, however, remain as the mark of Cain that continues to irk and pit Pilipinos of one faction or region against another.

Fr. Ximenez' status report to the King is amusing because of the way the population was categorized, "7,500 Indians---4000 belong to the king, 3,500 belong to encomenderos---600 Sangleys maintain 150 Sangley shops, 80 citizens, 13 clerics and 200 soldiers."

Spanish priests, like Fray Alonso Ximenez, were very important in the colonization of Pilipinas because the Spanish crown could not send sufficient number of secular personnel for the posts, especially those out in the boondocks. Outside of big cities, the friars did the tasks performed by ruling government officials, in addition to their duties as counselors and teachers of religion, which partly explains why Pilipinas is predominantly Roman Catholic. To sustain control with limited personnel, the Spaniards had to resort to divide-and-conquer tactics.

When America occupied Pilipinas they also resorted to the divide-and-conquer tactics to control the Pilipinos who resisted. For example, in order to capture General Emilio Aguinaldo and many other revolutionaries, the Americans used other Pilipinos who were ready and willing to betray their compatriots, even if that jeopardized the ideals of freedom and independence that Pilipinos were supposed to be all fighting for.

BARANGAY ACTIVITY

Make a list of the name of nations that have gotten their freedom by declaring independence from a former colonist. Don't hesitate to include Pilipinas.

SOURCES:
Otley H. Beyer, 1947. Philippine Saga: A Pictorial History of the Archipelago. Manila.
Renato Constantino, 1975, The Philippines: A Past Revisited. Quezon City: Renato Constantino.
John Leddy Phelan, 1959, The Hispanization of the Philippines. Madison: University of Wisconsin Press.

62

Y is for *Yamashita*

Gen. Tomoyuki Yamashita, the Tiger of Malaya, took over the command of the Japanese Imperial Army in Pilipinas in 1942, replacing Gen. Masaharu Homma. Japan occupied Pilipinas from 1942 through 1945 as part of the Greater East Asia Co-Prosperity Sphere, purportedly for the social economic development of all countries under Japan with the slogan "Asia for Asians!"

Japan was eventually defeated and in 1946 both Yamashita and Homma were tried by a military court for the atrocities committed by Japanese soldiers during the war. Both were found guilty and were executed by hanging in Los Baños.

Japan has played other parts in Pilipinas history, particularly as host for one of the revolutionary leaders. Gen. Artemio Ricarte chose to be banished by the Americans to Japan rather than serve under their regime. Ricarte believed that Japan helped to keep Pilipinas from exploitation by American imperialists.

Today, Japanese capital and business enterprises proliferate in the big city scenes. Besides being seen everywhere as tourists, the Japanese are seen and known to be buyers of prime property which are being converted into expensive resorts.

It is said that what influence the Japanese failed to capture by military effort in war, they now readily gain by economic maneuvering, with the usual Pilipino collaborator support.

The Bataan Death March began on April 1, 1942, with more than 60,000 Filipinos and 11,000 Americans who had surrendered to the Japanese. They were forced to hike to San Fernando, Pampanga, 120 kilometers away. From there, they were taken by train to Capas, Tarlac and were made to walk another 13 kilometers to Camp O'Donnell. The 54,000 who survived the march which was a nine day "phantasmagoria of swirling red dust, sweltering horses and moving men...crawling in the fierce sun" suffered added torture, brutality and neglect in the prison camp. By liberation day, only 4,000 Filipino and American prisoners greeted their liberators.

The Japanese occupying forces persuaded several of the Pilipino elites to collaborate and run a subservient Philippine Republic. In contrast, the peasants formed the Hukbalahap (*Hukbong Laban sa Hapon*) movement which opposed the Japanese military and their quisling cohorts. After the war, Americans regained government control and favored the Pilipino elites despite the cloud of collaboration and treason, deepening and prolonging the enmity of the *Huks* against the government.

Many confuse the *Huks* with the New People's Army, although at a few places they are one and the same. Lack of government credibility gives rise to dissident armies, peasant rebellions, as well as plain hooliganism.

BARANGAY ACTIVITY

List the brands of Japanese cars being sold. What other products do you know are made in Japan and are popular all over the world?

SOURCE:
   "War, Collaboration and Resistance" The Philippines Reader: A History of Colonialism, Neocolonialism, Dictatorship and Resistance. Daniel B. Schirmer & Stephen Rosskamm Shalom, Ed. Boston: South End Press, 1987.

A gunblast from an American soldier guarding the San Juan bridge sets off the Philippine American War, 1899-1901. Very few wars are actually planned but peace can be forged so that a new era of progress and harmony can provide opportunity for Filipino Americans, particularly, to help Pilipinas usher in a new dawn of fulfillment.

Z is for *Zapote*

Zapote was an insignificant town with a bridge linking the provinces of Cavite and Rizal. In 1897, Pilipino revolutionaries under Gen. Aguinaldo wiped out a well-armed contingent of Spanish soldiers trying to cross the bridge.

Another bridge---the one at San Juan---became famous, because on February 4, 1899, American soldiers guarding the bridge shot Pilipinos who ignored the order "Halt!" Thus started the Pilipino American war, which raged for about two years,

> The lure of American progress is close to impossible to resist. Pilipinos love things American. As soon as America settled to govern their country, Pilipinos began the steady migration to the United States. Beginning in 1906, thousands of farmworkers were siphoned as *sacadas* (harvesters) to fill American agribusiness labor needs, first in Hawaii and then in California.
>
> By 1955, with a new immigration policy, the U.S. encouraged skilled and professional Pilipinos to immigrate and constitute the brain drain. The desire to be in America is so strong that many Pilipinos risk being TNTs or *tago ng tago* (hide 'n hide) and be illegal residents, hoping beyond hope while hiding from authorities, to gain resident status and eventually U.S. citizenship.
>
> In the last decade, qualified Pilipino WWII veterans, many of them feeble septuagenarians responding to the offer of American citizenship, took advantage of a better-late-than-never response of the U.S. government to their having served in America's war in the Pacific.

making Mark Twain protest, "30,000 killed a million." A century later, that contest continues in claims of rights over hijacked church bells of Balangiga, Samar.

In less than a century of colonization, America taught democracy to Pilipinos. But needing to sift through heavy Spanish cultural load over their own, Pilipinos shall need greater opportunity to develop the democracy appropriate to their historical and cultural experience.

Methodically, American teachers, missionaries, merchants and carpetbaggers have been infecting Pilipinos with the bug of modernism. At the time of the arrival of the first American teachers known as Thomasites in 1901, the Presbyterian James B. Rodgers pioneered the protestant missionary movement, bringing Americanized churches, schools, hospitals and community development programs to goad Pilipinos into new social directions. Few are conscious though of how much low-grade Americana are gobbled up by Pilipinos through movies, TV, records and other popular media, promoting contestable values like individualistic materialism.

BARANGAY ACTIVITY

List the names of nations against whom the U.S. has waged war or invaded and list the reasons why.

SOURCES:

James H. Blount, 1913, American Occupation of the Philippines. New York: G. P. Putnam's Sons.

"Colonization" The Philippines Reader: A History of Colonialism, Neocolonialism, Dictatorship and Resistance D. Schirmer & Stephen Rosskamm Shalom, Ed. Boston: South End Press, 1987.

FORCES PROPELLING PILIPINAS TO NATIONHOOD

1. Mastery of the rice culture technology as used in building the terraces in the Mountain Provinces.
2. Mastery of boat building technology promoting migration and eventual implantation of barangay as socio-politial unit.
3. Trade with China and other neighboring countries.
4. Arrival of Muslims around 1280.
5. Coming of Europeans, beginning in 1521.
6. Spain colonizes the islands and names them in honor of the king, Felipe II.
7. Pilipinos partake in the Manila-Acapulco galleon trade; founded Manila villages in Louisiana and took part in Spanish emprise in California.
8. Pilipinos are Christianized.
9. Pilipinos witness Chinese presence in the Parian and affirm long-established ties as groundwork for permanent Chinese influence.
10. Pilipinos are introduced to the printing press.
11. Pilipinos experience the public school system established by Spaniards for Pilipinos and later developed by Americans.
12. Pilipino intellectuals taste freedom as students in European institutions.
13. Pilipinos witness the execution of Fathers Gomez, Burgos and Zamora.

14. Pilipinos read Jose Rizal's books, Noli me Tangere and El Filibusterismo.
15. Pilipinos witness the execution of Jose Rizal.
16. Pilipinos led by Andres Bonifacio found the Katipunan and stage the revolution against Spain.
17. Pilipinos led by Gen. Emilio Aguinaldo declare *Republika ng Pilipinas*, June 12, 1898.
18. Pilipinos fight the Pilipino American War, 1899-1901, are conquered and colonized by Americans; Pilipinos begin to migrate to the United States.
19. Pilipinos become part of American Commonwealth and legislate women's suffrage.
20. Pilipinos are conquered and occupied by Japan; in the wear for liberation, Pilipinos fight side-by-side with Americans and defeat the Japanese.
21. Pilipinos receive independence from America in 1946 , abolish tenancy and initiate land reform .
22. Pilipinos mandate Tagalog-based *wikang pambansa* or national language.
23. Pilipinos assert People Power, depose a dictator, and elect first woman president, 1986.
24. Pilipinos participate in formation of ASEAN community and assumes a stance in global economics.
25. Pilipinos regain control of bases formerly held by Americans,1994.
26. Pilipinos establish accord with Muslim communities through Autonomous Region of Muslim Mindanao (ARMM).

How to use the LEARNER'S GUIDE

Although this book was written with individual independent readers in mind, it can serve as a basis for programmed instruction. The following outline can be a basis for lesson planning:

    1. CHRONOLOGICAL SEQUENCE. The learner or instructor can track five major periods in Pilipino history:
        A. Prehistory
        B. Hispanization
        C. Pilipinization
        D. Americanization
        E. Globalization.

    2. CORRELATION OF TOPICS TO OUTLINE. Beyond providing a chronological outline, the LEARNER'S GUIDE, through questions related to specific topics, helps the learner to establish correlation between the individual topics and the five historical epochs. By attempting to answer the questions, the learner will be prompted to make the connections, thus showing how specific topics flow to form the historical stream.

    3. REVIEW. The LEARNER'S GUIDE also serves as a review. The questions have been designed so that they help the learner remember the most important items in each essay. If an instructor needs to develop a test, this aspect of the guide can be useful in framing questions.

    4. Each BARANGAY ACTIVITY is aimed at grounding the topics on practical daily concerns.

A. PREHISTORY EPOCH

1. Archipelago
   What advantages are there in being a nation with so many islands and so much sea?
2. Barangay
   What is the source of the word" barangay " and what does it refer to chiefly today?
3. Luzon
   Name three very important things in the island of Luzon not found elsewhere in Pilipinas.
4. Bisayas
   What contributions is the City of Cebu making to the development of Pilipinas?
5 Mindanao
   What cultural gifts can be expected from the various ethnic groups in the island of Mindanao?
6. Darangen
   Name other epics and their respective places where they are best known.
7. Narra
   What is the name of the grouping for the trees to which narra belongs?
8. Corregidor
   In what large body of water is the island of Corregidor located?
9. Sabong
   What native games are still being played today?
10. Ulog
    What value is the ulog to the community?
11. Vinta
    Is the vinta still of value as a means of transportation in Pilipinas today? In what way?

LEARNER'S GUIDE

B. HISPANIZATION EPOCH

1. **España**

   Where did the Spanish explorers first land in the archipelago they later named Las Islas Filipinas?

2. **Flores de Mayo**

   Name some celebration dances associated with the observation of a saint's day.

3. **Humabon**

   What was the ritual of friendship that Humabon had with Magellan?

4. **Intramuros**

   In what way did Intramuros help the Spaniards control the Pilipinas colony? In what way was it not helpful?

5. **Corregidor**

   Why did the Spaniards think that Corregidor would be important to the defense of the colony?

6. **Ximenez**

   Name the rivaling Pilipino groups and suggest ways to reconcile them.

7. **Barangay**

   Name the barangay chief who killed Ferdinand Magellan.

8. **GOMBURZA**

   Aside from church duties, what were some of the other responsibilities that had to be done by priests in the Spanish times?

9. **Gabriela**

   Who were some of the Pilipino women who featured prominently in the revolution?

C . PILIPINIZATION EPOCH

1. **Archipelago**

   Name some of the nations that were trading with Pilipinas long before the coming of Westerners.

2. **Barangay**

   Why has this ancient, original word remained in Pilipino use today?

3. **Gomburza**

   Give the full names of the three priests who were executed by the Spaniards. What Church declared itself independent of the Roman Catholic Church as result of the Pilipinas revolution?

4. **Gabriela**

   Make a list of outstanding Pilipino women today with their corresponding achievements.

5. **Katipunan**

   Say the full original name of the Katipunan. What three letters stand for the association?

6. **Ulog**

   From the community's point of view, what is the chief purpose of the ulog custom? What can be learned rom the ulog custom that will benefit married couples today?

7. **Mindanao**

   List some benefits derived by the people in Mindanao in having been models of resistance against invaders and keepers of the integrity of the customs of the people?

8. **Darangen**

   What good can be gained from beliefs in the supernatural---like the power of the anting-anting (good luck charm) or mangkukulam (vodoo)?

LEARNER'S GUIDE

D. AMERICANIZATION EPOCH

1. Zapote
How long did the Pilipino-American war last? What influence does the United States have over Pilipinas today?

2. Corregidor
What caused the loss of the strategic military value of the island of Corregidor?

3. Olongapo
What problems are faced by Pilipino children born of Pilipino mothers fathered by American servicemen?

4. Pinoy
How did the word *Pinoy* come about? What are some other words that are similar to *Pinoy*?

5. Quezon
What was President Manuel Quezon's main objective as a national leader? Name other nationalistic Pilipino leaders.

6. Republic
What chief features does the Pilipinas republic have in comparison to the United States?

7 Yamashita
What was Gen. Yamashita known for before he commanded the Japanese army in Pilipinas?

8. Metro Manila
What are some characteristics of Metro Manila that are typical of large cities?

E. GLOBALIZATION

1. Jeepney
What other forms of transporation are more effective than the *jeepney*? Explain why you believe so.

2. Metro Manila
Other than Manila, name other cities or districts that comprise Metropolitan Manila.

3. Narra
List three places where an environmental or conservation program is going on in Pilipinas.

4. Olongapo
In what ways are Pilipino women being exploited by foreigners today ?

5. Pinoy
List the names of countries where *Pinoys* are still going in significant numbers and explain why.

6. Taglish
Is Taglish preferable to pure Tagalog or pure English as a language for the nation?

7. Watawat
Draw the flag of Pilipinas from memory and learn to sing the *Pambasang Awit* with someone.

8. Republic
Name the three main divisions of government of the Republic of Pilipinas.

9. Sabong
Give some reasons why you would favor elimination of *sabong* in community life..

Suggested Readings

Santiago V. Alvarez, 1992, The Katipunan and the Revolution: Memoirs of a General. Manila: Ateneo de Manila University Press.

Miguel A. Bernard, S.J., 1982, Tradition and Discontinuity: Essays on Philippine History and Culture. MetroManila: National Bookstore

Emma Helen Blair & James Alexander Robertson, Ed., The Philippines Islands 1493-1898. Mandaluyong: Cacho Hermanos.

James H. Blount, 1913, American Occupation of the Philippines 1898-1912. New York: G.P. Putnam's Sons.

Renato Constantino, 1971, The Filipinos in the Philippines and Other Essays. Quezon City: Malaya Books, Inc.

Renato Constantino, 1975, The Philippines: A Past Revisited. Quezon City: Renato Constantino.

Renato Constantino & Letizia R. Constantino, 1978, The Philippines: The Continuing Past. Quezon City: Foundation of Nationalist Studies.

Fred Cordoba, 1983, Filipinos: Forgotten Asian Americans. Dubuque: Kendall/Hunt Publishing Co.

O.D. Corpuz, 1989, The Roots of the Filipino Nation, Vol. I & II. Quezon City: AKLAHI Foundation, Inc.

Austin Craig, 1933, The Filipino's Fight for Freedom. Manila: Oriental Commercial Co. Inc.

Duyan ng Magiting, Pacifico Aprieto, Ed. Quezon City, Instructional Materials Corp., 1989.

Filipino Heritage: The Making of a Nation, Alfredo R. Roces et al, Ed. Vol. 1-10. Manila: Lahing Pilipino Publishing Inc, 1977.

John Foreman, 1906, The Philippine Islands. New York: Charles Scribner's Sons.

Mariel N. Francisco & Fe Maria C. Arriola, 1987, The History of the Burgis. Quezon City: GCF Books.

Lewis E. Gleeck, Jr., 1986, The American Governors-General and High Commissioners in the Philippines. Quezon City: New Day Publishers.

Maria Odulio de Guzman, 1967, The Filipino Heroes. Manila: National Book Store.

Vic Hurley, 1938, Jungle Patrol: The Story of the Philippine Constabulary. New York: E.P. Dutton & Co, Inc.

F. Landa Jocano, 1975, Philippine Prehistory: An Anthropological Overview of the Beginnings of Filipino Society and Culture: Quezon City: Philippine Center for Advanced Studies, University of the Philippines.

Stanley Karnow, 1989, In Our Image. New York: Ballantine Books.

Elena G. Maquiso, 1994, Ulahingan: Epic of Southern Philippines. Series 1-4. Dumaguete City: Elena Maquiso & Toyota Foundation.

Vicente Marasigan, S.J., 1985. Quezon City: Ateneo de Manila University Press.

Howard P. McKaughan, 1995. Manila: De La Salle University Press, Inc.

Elly Velez Pamatong, 1992, American Birthright on Trial: Why Filipinos are Still U.S. Citizens or Nationals. San Francisco: Elly Velez Pamatong & Maria Torres Reyes.

Ruby R. Paredes, 1989, Philippine Colonial Democracy. Quezon City: Ateneo de Manila University Press.

John Leddy Phelan, 1959, Hispanization of the Philippines. Madison: University of Wisconsin Press

Manuel L. Quezon, 1946, The Good Fight: An Autobiography. New York: D. Appleton-Century, Co.

Francis St. Clair, 1902, The Katipunan: The Rise and Fall of the Filipino Commune. Manila: TIP Amigos del Pais, Palacio 258.

War, Collabortation and Resistance: The Philippines Reader, Daniel B. Schirmer, et. al, Ed. Boston: South End Press, 1987.

Joseph L. Schott, 1964, The Ordeal of Samar. Indianapolis: Bobbs Merrrill Co., Inc.

William Henry Scott, 1984, Prehispanic Source Materials for the Study of Philippine History. Manila: New Day Publishers.

Moorfield Storey & Marcial P. Lichauco, 1926, The Conquest of the Philippines by the United States, 1898-1925. New York: G.P. Putnam's Sons.

José P. Rizal, 1986 & 1891, Noli Me Tangere & El Filibusterismo (Translated by Ma. Soledad Lacson-Locsin). Makati City: Bookmark Inc.

T. Valentino Sitoy Jr., 1985, A History of the Philippines: Initial Encounter, Vol. 1. Quezon City: New Day Publishers.

Student's Philippine Almanac, Virgilio S. Almario et al, Ed. Makati: Children's Communication Center, 1991.

Ronald Takaki, 1994, Spacious Dreams: The First Wave of Asian Immigration. New York: Chelsea House Publishers.

Gregorio F. Zaide, 1984, Philippine History (Updated Edition). MetroManila: National Book Store.

MELCHIZEDEK MARAON SOLIS, D. Min., is the Grand Historian of the Caballeros de Dimasalang, the Executive Director of the National Filipino American Council, Monterey County Chapter, and Consultant for the Cultural Committee of the Filipino Community of Salinas Valley. He is a member of the Filipino American National Historical Society. His unpublished doctoral dissertation, "Barangay: A Filipino American Experience" has been adapted into a syllabus for Pilipino History and Culture and is a major resource for this introductory book. A correspondent of The Philippine News, he has been associate editor for The Asian American Times and The Philippine Press USA (succeeding the Philippines Mail which was founded by the Caballeros de Dimasalang in Salinas, California in 1922).

Dr. Solis is the author of Link: A Novel of Real Power and coeditor of *Itugyan*: The Life and Work of Zoe Rodriguez Lopez.

Ordained in the United Church of Christ in the Philippines and currently a minister of the Presbyterian Church, U.S.A., Dr. Solis volunteers as associate pastor of the Korean Glory Presbyterian Church in Salinas, California.

LEO BRAVO PARTIBLE is a film production assistant working in Los Angeles, California. Leo is also a singer/songwriter.

MELANIE SOLIS McKNIGHT directs the art department of the Household Credit Services, Inc. at its offices in Salinas, California.

REEV LOPEZ SOLIS is a free lance photographer and liaison for Graphic Print Arts in Salinas, California.